Portraits of HISPanic American Heroes

BY JUan FeLIPe Herrera

PAINTINGS BY RaúL COLóN

Dial Books for Young Readers An imprint of Penguin Group (USA) LLC

≈\\⁄⁄≈

"DON'T BE AFRAID TO REACH FOR THE STARS..."
—Ellen Ochoa, first Latina astronaut, La Mesa, California

"ALL THE BOYS ON HERO STREET COULD HARDLY WAIT TO SERVE OUR COUNTRY."
—Sonny Soliz, Silvis, Illinois

"VICTORIA SOTO WAS ONE IN A MILLION."
—Police Chief Gary MacNamara, Newtown, Connecticut

≈\\⁄⁄≈

DIAL BOOKS FOR YOUNG READERS
Published by the Penguin Group
Penguin Group (USA) LLC
375 Hudson Street, New York, New York 10014

USA / Canada / UK / Ireland / Australia / New Zealand / India / South Africa / China
penguin.com
A Penguin Random House Company

Text copyright © 2014 by Juan Felipe Herrera
Pictures copyright © 2014 by Raúl Colón

Library of Congress Cataloging-in-Publication Data

Herrera, Juan Felipe.
Portraits of Hispanic American heroes / by Juan Felipe Herrera ; pictures by Raul Colon.
pages   cm
Summary: "Twenty Hispanic American artists, scientists, athletes, activists and political leaders are profiled in this stunning picture
book, complete with inspirational quotes and distinctive expressionist portraits"—Provided by publisher.
ISBN 978-0-8037-3809-6 (hardback)
1. Hispanic Americans—Biography—Juvenile literature. I. Colón, Raúl, illustrator. II. Title.
E184.S75H486 2014   920.009268—dc23   [B]   2013044661

Manufactured in China on acid-free paper

1 3 5 7 9 10 8 6 4 2

Designed by Jasmin Rubero
Text set in Filosofia OT

*The illustrations are done on watercolor paper and combine watercolor washes,
etching, and the use of colored pencils and litho pencils.*

For my personal heroes, my mother, Lucha Quintana, a singer and poet who wrote her verses on scraps of paper and mesmerized me with our family's stories of survival during the Mexican Revolution; and my father, Felipe Emilio, a courageous man, who in the 1890s, at fourteen years of age, crossed the US–Mexican border and explored the wonders of the Southwest. For my sisters, Concha Contreras and Sara Chavez, and all my children, grand-children, and my giant *familia*. For my agent, Kendra Marcus, and editor, Lucia Monfried—thank you for your guidance and for believing in me. Raúl Colón, *gracias* for your art, making visible the heart of our heroes.

And in memory of my brother, David F. Herrera, and my brother-in-law, Bobby Robles. You are all heroes.

J. F. H.

For "Fightin" Makenzie—little big girl, welcome to your world.

R.C.

CONTENTS

$\mathcal{H}$EROES $\mathcal{U}$NDER THE $\mathcal{S}$UN AND $\mathcal{A}$CROSS THE $\mathcal{S}$TARS

A "hero," *un héroe,* was rarely in my vocabulary growing up as an only child of two tireless and kind California farmworkers. Speaking and reading only Spanish when I began school made my hero discoveries more difficult.

Yet, my library was rich with storytelling and other "oral" forms of history about Latina and Latino bravery, voyages, and experiments. And it still is the way many Hispanic Americans learn about their heroes. To this day, I sing the *corridos,* ballads of the Mexican *Revolución,* that *Mamá* taught me. And my *papí's* harmonica—I play it sweetly.

The Civil Rights Act of 1964 and the grape boycott led by César Chávez and Dolores Huerta roused a generation of Latina and Latino students, scholars, and community activists to ask: Are the stories about our Latino and Latina heroes, those who came or were born here in the United States, in our libraries? Most of the books had to be written. And they were—filled with lives in search of change, justice, and innovation—and a place they could call home. The books diamond-sparkled with unimaginable heroism.

David Farragut sailed the seas defending the Union, Desi Arnaz was exiled from Cuba. Judy Baca transformed a city with paint! Julia de Burgos arrived on the mainland with a sack of her power poetry about Puerto Rico. Because her skin was brown, Joan Baez figured out another way to become popular—and changed our lives. Adelina Otero-Warren fought for bilingual readers; Luis W. Alvarez crushed the armor of atoms; Roberto Clemente slammed his baseball bat for the world; Senator Dennis Chavez demanded civil rights before they were called "civil rights." Even in space boundaries had to be challenged—Ellen Ochoa leaped into the stars as the first Latina astronaut.

In a land of immigrants, it is an irony that Latino lives have been largely ignored. Although there have been incredible contributions by Hispanic Americans since the beginnings of this nation, their pioneering roles often have been overshadowed and their identities besmirched by terms such as "alien" and "illegal."

Crossing borders was a major theme in the lives of the extraordinary heroes in this book—and it is to this day. The boundaries of language still exist, but Hispanic Americans continue to make this nation flourish.

When Tomás Rivera gazed at his migrant family struggling in the fields, like mine, rather than smolder in anger, he noticed their unconquerable wisdom to seek out brilliant horizons—the roots of the hero. May you say *hero* in many languages. May you become one.

BERNARDO DE GÁLVEZ

BORN: JULY 23, 1746, IN MÁLAGA, SPAIN
DIED: NOVEMBER 30, 1786, IN NEW SPAIN (MEXICO TERRITORY)

Born in Macharaviaya, a mountain village in Málaga, Spain, to a military family, young Bernardo followed his father and uncles into the Spanish royal service. In 1762, at the age of sixteen, he began as a lieutenant in the Spanish army, posted to Portugal, then he fought in New Spain (Mexico territory) and North Africa.

In 1776, the year that the thirteen American colonies declared independence from Britain, Gálvez was transferred to the distant province of Louisiana in the new world. The Louisiana Territory, an immense expanse of land, at that time belonged to Spain. It controlled land as far as the Mississippi River, while the British controlled the land along the East Coast and had several posts at the southern end of the colonies.

In Europe, Spain was an ally of France; both were enemies of Great Britain. In the colonies, Gálvez pursued Spain's interests, which served the American cause. Gálvez was familiar with the area along the Mississippi River and the Gulf Coast from his previous postings there. He corresponded directly with American leaders, including Patrick Henry and Thomas Jefferson, and sent bullets, supplies, medicine, and arms up the Mississippi River to aid the colonists. He claimed the town of New Orleans for Spain and drove the British out of the Gulf of Mexico. This meant that American, Spanish, and French ships (France also favored the American colonists) could travel up the Mississippi River to reach the American forces in the north.

Once Spain actually entered the war against the British in 1779, Gálvez could engage officially with the British. Always keen on strategy and with the needs of his troops in mind, he arranged for the transfer of cattle from Texas to provide meat for those under his command nearly a century before the great cattle drives out of Texas. Gálvez also requested several hundred horses for his cavalry, and he did not hesitate to share these resources with American forces. Young and dashing—he was in his early thirties at the time—he forged ahead with his own battle plans, even without the support of other Spanish leaders. Thus he became known as *Yo Solo*, "I alone."

He gathered troops that were a mixture of Spaniards, mixed-race Creoles, Mexicans, and Native Americans. With these reinforcements, his 1,400 soldiers were able to defeat the British in battles in Manchac, Baton Rouge, and Natchez. They next captured Mobile, thus overtaking all the major Southern British strongholds except Pensacola. His most important victory was to come there.

"YO SOLO,"
"I ALONe"

In 1781, just months before the British defeat at Yorktown, Virginia—which ended with their ultimate defeat in the war—Gálvez took the large British outpost in Florida in what has become known as the Siege of Pensacola. It has been called by historians one of the most brilliantly executed battles of the war, the one that broke the back of the British.

A year later he made the last of his contributions to the American Revolution—he was among a select group that drafted the terms of the Treaty of Paris that ended the war.

He returned to Spain with his family, but in 1785, he was appointed as Viceroy to New Spain, succeeding his father. Always the compassionate and caring leader, upon his move to Mexico City which was undergoing a famine, he gave away much of his personal fortune to provide for the people in need. He died suddenly at the age of forty.

The city of Galveston on the Texas coast is named for this hero. While Gálvez was still governor of Louisiana, the body of water now known as Galveston Bay was called *Bahía de Galveston.*

In 1976, for the American Bicentennial, Spain gave to the United States a statue of Bernardo de Gálvez astride a horse in a triumphant gait, which stands on Virginia Avenue in Washington, D.C. Presenting the statue, the king of Spain said: "May the statue of Bernardo de Gálvez serve as a reminder that Spain offered the blood of her soldiers for the cause of American independence."

The inscription at the base reads: "Bernardo de Gálvez, the great Spanish soldier carried out a courageous campaign in lands bordering the lower Mississippi. This masterpiece of military strategy lightened the pressure of the English against the American settlers who were fighting for their independence."

DAVID GLASGOW FARRAGUT

BORN: JULY 5, 1801, NEAR CAMPBELL'S STATION, TENNESSEE
DIED: AUGUST 14, 1870, IN PORTSMOUTH, NEW HAMPSHIRE

A log cabin in the thick green forests of Cherokee and Creek Indian country, near Knoxville, Tennessee, was the first home of David Glasgow Farragut, the first admiral of the United States Navy. The log house that his father, who was born in Spain, built still stands to this day. Strength was part of David's character. And he would inherit the courage of his mother, who was known to stand at the door with an ax to protect her children from intruders.

The family moved to New Orleans, where his mother died of yellow fever shortly thereafter. Seven-year-old James (as he was then known) waved *adiós* to his father and his two brothers and two sisters. He took the hand of his father's friend and associate, David Porter, a commander in the U.S. Navy, left for Washington, and became the adopted son of the Porter family. He took on a new name, David, after his adoptive father, and a new family—the Navy. He never saw his real father again. That same year Commander Porter appointed young David to the rank of midshipman.

Boys headed for naval careers were taken aboard ships at a young age. And so he went to sea. David set sail with his adopted father on the *Essex* where he came face-to-face with life on a man-of-war. Food was rationed to such a degree that for months only half a pound of bread was served daily. At the age of twelve, he received his first promotion. Because of his age and size, it was not unusual for older officers to challenge him. But he was known, due to his bravado, as a lad made up of "three pounds of uniform and seventy pounds of fight."

Fearless, confident, and kind, he deepened his knowledge of crews, ships, and shores and earned the respect of his men. He fought against the British in 1815 and served in the Caribbean from 1815 to 1820.

In the 1820s Farragut arrived in Norfolk, Virginia, where for the next four decades he would serve ashore at the Norfolk Navy Yard. He was promoted to commander and left for a time to supervise the construction of a Navy yard on Mare Island, San Francisco—the first one on the Pacific Coast. He was in charge of the remodeling, repairing, and building of Navy ships.

The Mexican War in 1846 pulled Farragut into action. In 1847 he collected a crew and sailed south in the sloop of war *Saratoga* to fight in that war.

But changes were coming to the nation. Shortly after Abraham Lincoln was elected president in 1860, he abolished slavery in the United States. South Carolina seceded from the Union, and Mississippi, Florida, Georgia, Louisiana, and

"DAMN THE TORPEDOES! FULL SPEED AHEAD!"

Texas followed. Farragut, born in Tennessee and now a Virginian, felt divided. Nevertheless, he decided to remain faithful to the Union. Secession, for David, was treason. He could not denounce the government that had cared for him since childhood and given him his naval education, his ships, and his crews. In the Civil War that followed, David Farragut achieved his greatest fame as a courageous leader.

In command of a military force of fifteen thousand men, Farragut set sail on the USS *Hartford* in April, 1862, to take the city and port of New Orleans. After the defeat of the Confederates there, Congress honored Farragut with a rank specifically created for him, as rear admiral.

Two years later, on August 5, 1864, Farragut won another great victory. Mobile, Alabama, was the Confederacy's last major port on the Gulf of Mexico. Although Mobile Bay was heavily laced with tethered naval mines known as *torpedoes,* Farragut, with his eighteen ships, charged the bay. Now sixty-three years old, he lashed himself to the rig. His lead ship, *Tecumseh*, was sinking; the ship ahead, the *Brooklyn*, was stalling. "What's the trouble?" Farragut shouted through his trumpet. Torpedoes! He did not look back. "Damn the torpedoes! Full speed ahead!" he shouted. The Confederates were defeated in the Battle of Mobile Bay. Farragut lost only one ship.

On December 21, 1864, David Glasgow Farragut was promoted to full admiral, a rank created for him. He was the first. Two years later he declined to run for president of the United States.

Adelina Otero-Warren

BORN: OCTOBER 23, 1881, IN LOS LUNAS, NEW MEXICO
DIED: JANUARY 3, 1965, IN SANTA FE, NEW MEXICO

Adelina Otero-Warren was the first *Hispana* to run for Congress from New Mexico. She was born in a grand house—*La Luna Mansion*—much like a plantation of the American South, on a vast expanse of a land given by the Spanish decades earlier to her family. They were wealthy and influential.

Baby Nina, as she was called as a child, was loud. "Nina wanted to be the boss . . . she had the brains of the family," people recalled. She wanted to fight—and her fight ended up *for the rights of women and children*.

At the age of eleven, Adelina was sent to school in St. Louis; two years later, like other Catholic females of that time and place, her education was over. Back in New Mexico, she conducted lessons for her eleven younger siblings; she continued to teach and advise them all through her life. When she was sixteen, the family moved to Santa Fe. She thrived in the city as part of her large and active clan. At the center of many of the town's social activities and as the first woman member of the Santa Fe school board, Adelina's mother was a strong role model for her daughter. When she died in 1914 Adelina assumed her position on the school board and vowed to become a professional career woman. She hired a governess to care for her younger siblings, managed the family finances, and took on the school board job with gusto.

Despite her own limited education, Adelina was appointed by the governor as superintendent of public schools in Santa Fe in 1917. The next year she ran for the post and kept it until 1929. Even when she was young and inexperienced, she began shaking things up with the idea of change—change the schools, make them bilingual, change the teaching, change the books, and include Spanish texts. No more punishment for speaking Spanish in class or on the playground. Increase schooltime to nine months, raise teachers' salaries and provide more training, mix English classes with other programs, and teach the arts in Spanish. She pushed for more girls in all schools. Although her own education had terminated at a young age, she held the belief that more education meant more leadership opportunities and, sooner or later, the right to participate equally in the political process.

At this time in U.S. history, women could not vote. But votes for women was a cause Adelina took up in her home state. The suffragist, Alice Paul, leader of the National Women's Party, credited Adelina with successful lobbying to pass the Nineteenth Amendment into the constitution of New Mexico. In 1920, it officially became part of the U.S. Constitution—women won the right to vote.

"we WILL win."

Now that women had the vote, they could enter politics. In 1922, at the age of forty-one,

18

Adelina decided to run for a Republican seat in Congress, the first woman in New Mexico to do so. But people got wind that Adelina had been divorced from a military officer to whom she had been married for a short time in her twenties. During these times, women were looked down upon for not staying married. Her opponents used this against her and she lost the election. So she turned her attention back to her job as superintendent of education in Santa Fe.

The education of children in rural areas and Native American children was also important to her. Rebuild the Indian schools, stop separating children from their parents so that they could attend non-reservation schools, provide more educational materials and possibilities for mothers, include the history and life stories of Native American people in schoolbooks and classrooms! Adelina demanded.

In 1929, Adelina retired from public service and retreated to her ranch to write. But as part of the New Deal of President Franklin D. Roosevelt, Otero-Warren was appointed as Director of Literacy for New Mexico's Civilian Corps, and in 1941 she was appointed Director of Adult Literacy in Puerto Rico. There she noticed the crumbling schools, the scorched recreation areas, and the few dusty books. Once again, Adelina pushed for the same kind of educational reforms she had always fought for in New Mexico.

Passionate about her beliefs throughout her life, this scion of a New Mexico family fought for women and children. She sought a better education for all, and also to include the Spanish cultural values of so many in her region.

IGnacIO E. Lozano

BORN: 1886, IN MARIN, NUEVO LEÓN, MEXICO
DIED: SEPTEMBER 21, 1953, IN LOS ANGELES, CALIFORNIA

Through brambles, briars, and baking desert heat, twenty-two-year-old Ignacio E. Lozano escaped from Mexico with his family to *El Norte,* the United States. With a few bags of *pan dulce,* sundry takings, and the clothes he was wearing, he survived the harsh journey from his small pueblo in Nuevo León, with his widowed mother, Alicia, and five sisters. They arrived in San Antonio, Texas, a city right on the border with Mexico in 1908.

Two years later the Mexican Revolution exploded in full force with a call to depose the president, who was trying to modernize Mexico and form closer ties to the rich country to the north, and was taking land away from small farmers and causing terrible hardship.

Along with other refugees fleeing injustice into Texas, young Ignacio wondered about his village, friends, and family. So he opened his own bookstore and met other exiles. With Adolfo D. Salinas, a publisher, Ignacio worked on two Spanish-language periodicals, and then another paper, *El Imparcial de Texas.* Ignacio became an editor and a journalist—a man interested in reporting on a country falling apart, his country. His countrymen were Spanish-speaking people, and they needed to read a newspaper in their own language.

21

After learning the publishing trade from these early efforts, Ignacio decided in 1913 that it was time to launch his own independent newspaper—*La Prensa*. Rather than print the usual local fare, he took courageous steps as a young journalist. He published weekly articles on battles and changes in Mexico—the new leaders, the return of the land to the poor, riots. Two years later, *La Prensa* was a daily, printing reports on the lives of political refugees, those in flight from Mexico to the United States, as well as events in Mexico, too.

Even though the Mexican revolution was over by the 1920s, Lozano's paper was passionate about the issues of justice, land reform, and equality for people in Mexico. Ignacio wanted the truth to be told, he wanted an informed and honest voice to be heard across Texas and Mexico. And because of his coverage on such issues, *La Prensa* was censored more than once in Mexico. That did not stop him. He hired serious thinkers and writers. He employed direct correspondents in Paris, Mexico City, and Washington. His family had suffered in Mexico and crossing the border. Others were still suffering. Reporting on this could make it possible for difficult topics to be talked about in schools, bus stations, and kitchens.

As his publishing business grew in San Antonio, Ignacio noticed that similar migrations of *Mexicanos* had flowed across Mexico to California, and many had settled in Los Angeles. After shipping his newspaper to that southern California city by train, and having it read days late, he decided it was time to

"GENTLE WAYS DON'T WEAKEN VALOR."

inaugurate a new Spanish-language paper in Los Angeles. News has to be new!

Ignacio chose a newsworthy day: on the celebration of Mexican Independence Day, September 16, in 1926, Ignacio E. Lozano established *La Opinión* in the heart of Los Angeles, next to City Hall. His wife, Alicia, also from Nuevo León, whom he had married in 1921, took charge of *La Prensa* in San Antonio, while Ignacio managed the daily operations of *La Opinión*.

His son, Ignacio Jr., remembers how every evening after dinner, Ignacio Sr. took him to the final print of the next day's issue. There, he reminded Ignacio Jr. how to steady the grippers onto the paper, check the boilerplate, and let the rollers of the printing press rumble out the paper's name in capital letters—LA OPINIÓN. He was establishing a newspaper dynasty. His son took over the publishing of the paper upon his death.

In 1928, the Congress of the Latin Press recognized Lozano Sr.'s powerful journalism against political corruption. In 1953, shortly before he died, he was lauded by the leadership of San Antonio, Texas, for his civic accomplishments—on the fortieth anniversary of his first paper, *La Prensa*.

Today, his grandchildren manage *La Opinión*, still the largest Spanish-language newspaper in the United States.

Dennis "DIONISIO" CHavez

BORN: APRIL 8, 1888, IN LOS CHAVEZ, NEW MEXICO TERRITORY
DIED: NOVEMBER 18, 1962, IN WASHINGTON, D.C.

Dee-yon-sneez-ee-oh? The kids at the English-language Presbyterian Mission School in Albuquerque, New Mexico, made fun of Dionisio's Spanish name. "Let's call you Dennis," the teacher suggested. And so young Dionisio became Dennis. Dionisio had met tougher challenges—such as leaving Los Chavez, the small town in the central New Mexico territory (New Mexico was not yet a state) where he had been born, to come with his parents and seven brothers and sisters to Albuquerque. "Dennis" was *muy bien*—just fine—if it helped him and his family. So he agreed.

Dennis later agreed to quit school at the age of thirteen to work as a grocery clerk. It was a sacrifice he was willing to make if it meant helping to feed his family. For the next five years Dennis delivered bags and boxes six days week. He studied and read at night, learning surveying. Then in 1906 he was hired by the city of Albuquerque and advanced to assistant engineer. Chavez was happy to take a job in civil service.

Working for the city tossed Dennis onto the stage of city politics. His father, David, had been a loyal lieutenant for the Republican leader, but the teenage Chavez didn't see that the Republicans were doing things to better anyone's living conditions—his own, his family's, or the larger *Hispano* population. Plus, he loved Thomas Jefferson and what he stood for. So he joined the Democratic Party. This was not an easy thing to do as most Hispanics were registered Republicans.

In 1908 Dennis started out giving speeches to the Hispanic communities in Gallup, New Mexico, and other towns for a Hispanic congressional candidate and translating English into Spanish for Democratic candidates. After years of organizing and campaigning for numerous candidates, in 1916, Chavez left his city job and ran for public office, as Bernalillo county clerk. Though Chavez lost the election, he gained the attention of the Democratic leadership. Senator A. A. Jones, for whom he had campaigned in 1916, offered him a position as a clerk for the U.S. Senate.

Now in Washington, Chavez resumed his education and was admitted to the law school at Georgetown University. During the day he worked in the Capitol and by night he attended classes at the school.

In 1920, Chavez returned to Albuquerque with a law degree in hand, eager to open up his own law practice. He re-entered politics two years later, winning election to the state House of Representatives. There the Republicans held the power. Frustrated with their agenda in favor of cattle and oil barons and the Santa Fe and Southern Pacific railroad conglomerates, he left after serving one term.

"DEMOCRACY MUST BELONG TO ALL OF US."

Along with others, Dennis recognized

the need for more Hispanic representation, so in 1930 he decided to run for national office. New Mexico elected him to the House of Representatives; having such a small population, New Mexico had only one representative. Then he set his sights on the U.S. Senate. In 1935 he was appointed by the governor of New Mexico to take over the seat of the sitting senator who had just died. He was elected the following year, the first of four terms he would serve. Under harsh criticism Chavez pushed for his ideals: "Either we are all free or we fail."

Chavez's vision was fearless—he introduced the first bill to protect Indian rights, citizenship, voting rights, and self-determination; he supported President Franklin Roosevelt's New Deal legislation, and he worked closely with Roosevelt on the development of the Pan-American Highway. In 1944 he introduced the bill for which he would be best known. It was called the Fair Employment Practices Commission Bill, prohibiting discrimination based on race, religion, color, national origin, or ancestry. Although the bill was defeated, twenty years later this idea would flower into the groundbreaking Civil Rights Bill of 1964.

At a time when being Mexican or Hispanic was regarded with contempt by fellow lawmakers, Chavez devoted his energy to the service of his country, state, and party, with little regard to the derision and discourtesy his ethnicity evoked. When he died in 1962, Dennis Chavez was fourth-ranking in Senate seniority. He was the first native-born Hispanic elected to the U.S. Senate and the second Hispanic to do so in its history. Starting in the 1920s, *Dionisio* Chavez opened doors for Latinos and Latinas in the political process.

LUIS W. ALVAREZ

BORN: JUNE 13, 1911, IN SAN FRANCISCO, CALIFORNIA
DIED: SEPTEMBER 1, 1988, IN BERKELEY, CALIFORNIA

As a child, Luis stared at clouds, mulled over microscopes, and used tools as toys. Then, he asked very simple questions: "What is this for? How does that work? How come that happened when I did that?" Why, why, why?

Luis never stopped asking questions—not even after he was awarded the Nobel Prize in Physics. His entire life as a scientist and engineer was guided by an insatiable thirst for knowledge—whether he got it from books, libraries, or teams of highly curious like-minded people.

Luis was born and grew up in San Francisco where his father, Walter, was a physiologist by day, a medical doctor in the evenings. His father loved to read books in his reading chair, close his eyes and try to think of new problems to solve. This became Luis's love, too. He was always searching for ways to solve puzzles.

By the time Luis was ten he could operate all of the small tools in his father's shop, and wire up the electrical circuits. In high school, he won an apprenticeship in the instrument shop of the Mayo Clinic in Rochester, Minnesota, where the family had moved. These early interests in mechanics and mechanical systems continued throughout his life, and he patented over twenty inventions.

Luis attended the University of Chicago, where he received his PhD degree in 1936, and then headed back to California. For the young scientist, his favorite questions began with "Why?" Why are electrons captured? Why do neutrons move so fast? Why does energy spin inside a helium bubble? Then, Luis would ask, "How?" How can I smash an atom? How can I scan a microwave? How can I land a jet in the dark?

Books, libraries, and research were so much of Luis's life that his science team friends called him the "walking card catalog" because he had read all the books in the science section of the research library and could find any article and book by memory.

Alvarez contributed to a number of radar projects, from early improvements to Identification Friend or Foe (IFF) radar beacons, now called transponders, to a system for preventing enemy submarines from realizing that they had been found by the new airborne microwave radars.

In the physics department at the University of California at Berkeley, he met other young scientists, among them Robert Oppenheimer. Oppenheimer headed up the large, varied, and extraordinary team that developed the atomic bomb for the United States that was dropped on Japan to end World War II. Oppenheimer recruited the most brilliant scientists in America to work together on the top-secret project, and Alvarez joined with other physicists, chemists, and engineers in Los Alamos, New Mexico. Though he was greatly

"HEROES HAVE BEEN IMPORTANT TO MY DEVELOPMENT AS A SCIENTIST."

saddened by the casualties that resulted after the dropping of the bomb, he firmly believed that nuclear technology would prevent more wars and innumerable deaths.

The Nobel Prize—which Alvarez received many years later, in 1968—was awarded to him for his research on the construction of a hydrogen "bubble chamber." This new high-energy technology allowed scientists to look inside the atom in a detailed fashion, an outcome of his research during WWII at Los Alamos. Luis also garnered many other awards, such as the Einstein Award and the National Medal of Science, and he was inducted into the National Inventors Hall of Fame.

Some of Luis's major inventions involved national security, such as creating the first submarine radar warning systems and inventing with his team the Ground-Controlled Approach that allows aircraft to land at night and in conditions of poor visibility. This system was used for many years, and saved countless lives. After WWII, he designed the first proton linear accelerator, which pulverized atoms into even tinier pieces.

Luis Walter Alvarez dedicated his life's work to physics, but he didn't hesitate to jump into a new field if it interested him. He X-rayed one of the Egyptian pyramids to determine if there were hidden chambers. And with his geologist son, Walter, and other colleagues, he proposed that the extinction of the dinosaurs resulted from an asteroid striking the earth. This type of constant questioning, flexibility in delving into new areas, and belief in science for the power of good is what made Luis W. Alvarez stand out.

JULIA DE BURGOS

BORN: FEBRUARY 17, 1914, IN CAROLINA, PUERTO RICO
DIED: JULY 6, 1953, IN NEW YORK, NEW YORK

With a poet's eye, Julia gazed over the heights down to the river of Barrio Santa Cruz, a poor neighborhood of Carolina, Puerto Rico. Then she would trek down the mountain into the city to exchange fruits and vegetables the family grew for supplies and cash.

Teachers loved this tall, rugged, cinnamon-colored, skinny girl. And they loved that Julia was always reading, reading, reading—and writing poems. Despite the hardships of her childhood, she savored her parent's stories-on-the-road and fairy tales by the river. The fragrant thick-leaved plants, flowers, and rivers of the *jíbaro* countryside brought her calm and solace. In due time, these moments and stories would flow from her own poetry. She would come to be known throughout the nation, Cuba, and the mainland as one of Puerto Rico's greatest poets, orators, and fiercest advocates for an independent Puerto Rico.

At the age of fourteen, Julia's father sold their land and moved the family to Río Piedras, where she won a scholarship to attend the university's high school. Once enrolled, she excelled in mathematics, science, and English. Julia ran track, swam, and played basketball. And, always wrote poetry. She skipped grades, receiving the highest marks, and in 1931 entered the University of Puerto Rico where she studied Education. She joined political student groups, and discussions raised there about the plight of Puerto Rico caught her attention. The more she thought and learned, the more she found herself in agreement with writers and political thinkers who believed that an independent Puerto Rico free of foreign rulers would better serve its families and children.

At the age of nineteen, she graduated from the university with honors as an elementary school teacher. However, the Great Depression of the 1930s had engulfed the world, and Julia had to take a series of jobs—working in a milk station offering free breakfasts to children, and then as a schoolteacher.

In her early twenties Julia traveled through Puerto Rico in a bus selling handmade flyers featuring the poem that later would make her famous—about her favorite river and the people of Puerto Rico—*"Río Grande de Loíza."* At the same time Julia began to publish the poems she eagerly jotted on paper or quickly completed on a borrowed typewriter. Before her twenty-fifth birthday, Julia composed and published her first two poetry collections, *Poem of 20 Furrows* and *Song of the Simple Truth.* Her work appeared in journals, flyers, and newspapers.

All the while she burned with the idea of an independent Puerto Rico free of foreign rulers. At the age of twenty-two, Julia delivered a speech, "Women Facing the Pain of the Nation," calling upon the women of Puerto Rico to join the ranks of those who believed in Puerto Rico's independence. Suddenly, Julia, the poet, took

"I was my own road."

a leap from the page and became a participant in the independence movement of Puerto Rico.

The mid-1930s was an explosive moment in the history of the island. There were demonstrations, brutal crackdowns, and protests. The police in the town of Ponce opened fire on a parade of marchers, and Julia rose up for the *independencia* cause, with ready pen and with her voice full of spirit and hope for change and freedom.

A year after winning the Institute of Puerto Rican Literature's Poetry Prize, Julia moved to New York City to work for a progressive Latino newspaper. At the end of that year she took off for Cuba in a romantic relationship and studied at the university, but returned to New York alone.

Between the years 1939 to 1953 Julia worked as a journalist and reporter, writing in weekly papers and continuing to write poetry. "Where is the voice of freedom?" her final poem of 1953 asked. In her last decade, Julia spoke about the future of Latin America, where all the races would be united. She called this amazing world, "*el Continente Mestizo*," the Mestizo Continent, a place of many cultures—indigenous, European, African. But by this time, both her mental and physical health began to fail. She died of pneumonia in a New York City hospital and was buried in a pauper's grave. Years later, her body was returned with garlands and honors to her island of Puerto Rico.

A lyric poet of her beloved Carolina landscapes and rivers, and a heartfelt orator for an independent Puerto Rico, Julia wrote tirelessly. She was her own road, and the road for her land and people.

Desi Arnaz

Born: March 2, 1917, in Santiago, Cuba
Died: December 2, 1986, in Hollywood, California

At age sixteen, Desiderio Arnaz y de Acha escaped Cuba with his father and landed in Key West, Miami. "*Plátanos!* Bananas!" he called as he sold fruit on the street in his new home. He sold broken tiles, too, and lived in a warehouse where he had to shoo away rats at night. Desi (a nickname later given to him in the Army) was an *exile* now.

No more would he be the wealthy teen from Santiago de Cuba, his birthplace. Everyone there knew the Arnaz y de Acha family line—his father and paternal grandfather had both been mayors of the city. His mother's side of the family were the founders of the world famous Bacardí Rum Company of Cuba. All that was lost during the Batista *Revolución* of 1933.

In his new country, Desi managed to smile, even sing. In his autobiography, he wrote: ". . . every time things are really terrible, I laugh." It was his secret: his quick and uncanny ability to adapt to changes, no matter how big. So he dug into his roots for a new kind of *revolución*— his *Cubano* identity in a new land.

Still a teenager, with his old guitar in hand, he joined a makeshift band—the Siboney Septet (even though it only had five musicians). There weren't many Cubans in Miami in those years, and the music they played with traditional Afro-Cuban instruments—a conga, *bongós,* and a *marímbula* (a wooden box with four metal strips above a hole in the middle)—was unfamiliar. He had to figure out a way to introduce the audience to a sound they never heard—*La Rumba Cubana.*

With his good looks and Latin flair, he was noticed by Xavier Cugat, the King of Latin Music, and went to sing with his band in New York. But after a brief stay Desi returned to Miami Beach to form his own group. The only problem was that few musicians except Desi knew how to play Latin music. But then he remembered the open-air musical *carnavales* of Santiago. Desi snapped on his conga and gave his band a tiny *carnaval* tutorial. People formed a line, popped to the beat, kicked their feet to the side. In no time, the "Conga Line Dance" became a national craze. Desi's *revolución* was catching on, with *cultura Cubana* bouncing out smiles, rhythm, dance, and song.

In the summer of 1939, Desi was picked for a romantic Latino role in the musical, *Too Many Girls.* With his huge self-confidence (he had never seen a Broadway show), he became an immediate hit. The reviews were so positive that he was brought to Hollywood to take part in the film version of the show. His co-star in the show was a young comedian, Lucille Ball. A year later they married.

"since I was very young I have always worked hard at whatever I have had to do."

Desi was on his way to the peak of show business success—in musicals, films, and comedy. After his stint in the Army in 1943, he was a movie star now netting $100,000 a year. Lucy and Desi were each popular in different spheres of the entertainment industry. She was the star of a successful radio show called *My Favorite Husband*, where she created the wacky character that would later become one of the most beloved in entertainment. CBS executives wanted to re-create something like it for the new medium of television, and she insisted that she would only do it if she brought her own husband along. Together they created the most popular, longest top-rated TV show of the 1950s—*I Love Lucy*. On the show, Desi played the Cuban bandleader married to ditzy scatterbrained Lucy.

There were questions from producers and sponsors: Is a Latino character married to a white woman acceptable on national television? Yes. They brought that to American audiences. She was the star, but he made the important creative decisions for the show. Before *I Love Lucy*, sitcoms were not filmed in front of a live audience. He changed that. He rented a run-down movie stage big enough to hold audiences and multiple stages. He filmed the live show so it could be viewed nationally. He used the multicamera setup for the first time and created the rerun.

By the end of the decade, Desi Arnaz was one of the richest and most powerful television producers, and with Lucy, co-founder and co-owner of Desilu Studios—with twenty-six soundstages and forty-three acres of back lot, more than any other studio in Hollywood. Desilu went on to produce some of the most popular shows of the 1950s and '60s.

Desi's *revolución* could be seen in everyone's living room. He changed American television—behind the scenes and on the screen.

César Estrada Chávez

BORN: MARCH 31, 1927, IN YUMA, ARIZONA
DIED: APRIL 23, 1993, IN SAN LUIS, ARIZONA

By the time César Chávez was ten years old, he had attended more than thirty schools. It was 1937, the decade of the Great Depression, and work was scarce when César's parents lost their home in Yuma, Arizona, and had to take to the roads. They joined hundreds of thousands of migrant workers that followed the crops in California. After school César and his buddies fished in the canals and cut mustard greens for meals. There was no money for clothes or food or transportation. César and his brother would take the silver aluminum from discarded cigarette packages until they had enough to make a big ball of foil, which they sold to a Mexican junk dealer to buy tennis shoes and two sweatshirts. It was a life of intense hardship. César never liked school—schools were segregated, and speaking Spanish was not allowed. César stopped going in the eighth grade to help the family.

At the age of nineteen, he joined the Navy and spent two years in the Western Pacific, then returned to California in 1948 and married.

For the next ten years, César learned the art of community organizing, talking to groups and teaching them how they could work together to better themselves. But in 1962, Cesar decided to return to the fields. The workers needed more than just a better salary. They needed insurance, medical assistance, a credit union, and support in translating Spanish into English— and their cause needed a leader.

He traveled from camp to camp, "planting an idea," about their rights and about his dream to form a union to protect them, like a family that helps one another. "Friends, let us act like one family," he said. Another organizer, Dolores Huerta, joined him and became a leader alongside César. Yet building a union of farmworkers was a challenge. As hard as he strived to convince the migrants to follow his example and speak out for their rights, he found that most were afraid of losing the only thing they had—their jobs. But Chávez and Huerta did not give up.

In Delano, California, on César's birthday in 1962, his cousin raised a homemade flag in front of 287 farmworkers. It was painted with a black eagle rising from a hot-red field of land. This was the beginning of *"La Causa,"* the National Farm Workers Association (NFWA), that later would become the United Farm Workers Union, a powerful organization to help migrant workers make a better life for themselves in the United States.

"I Traveled around, planting an idea."

Three years later, in 1965, César and his 1,200 NFWA families voted to join a strike against the Delano-area growers. This was the beginning of a five-year grape boycott. The following year, during spring, César and a small team of strikers made a historic march—a 340-mile *peregrinación,* or pilgrimage, from Delano to the steps of the state capitol in Sacramento to attract attention from the media, the politicians, and the public about *La Causa.* On the twenty-fifth day of marching, with a line of 10,000 sun-scorched people, César and the NFWA arrived. *¡Viva la Causa!* Long live the Cause! Schenley Industries growers scrambled for an agreement with the NFWA—the first union contract between a grower and farmworkers in U.S. history.

¡Huelga! Strike! On August 3, 1967, the farmworkers called a strike against the largest of the grape growers, who brought in strike breakers and the Teamsters Union. There were beatings, arrests, shootings. But violence was not part of César's plan. He had read about achieving goals through peaceful protest. César went back to Delano and made a vow: He would not eat until the workers would end violent clashes and act as one *familia.* Twenty-one days later, César, frail and trembling, ended the fast. By this time more than fifteen million Americans had joined the grape, lettuce, and Gallo wine boycott. He fasted again in the coming years in support of nonviolence and to protest the harmful effects of pesticides on workers.

Finally, in 1975, the landmark Agricultural Labor Relations Act was signed into law, a guarantee that California farmworkers had the right to organize and bargain with their employers.

César Chávez never owned a car, a house, or had a good-paying job; he devoted his life to assisting thousands to receive just wages and safer working conditions.

HeLen RODriGUeZ-TrIas

BORN: 1929 IN NEW YORK, NEW YORK
DIED: DECEMBER 27, 2001, IN NEW YORK, NEW YORK

¡Independencia! **Independence for** Puerto Rico! Helen shouted as she marched with a student faction of Puerto Rico's Nationalist Party through the campus grounds of the University of Puerto Rico in the late 1940s. *¡Huelga!* On strike! She joined the students in response to the barring of a Nationalist leader as a speaker. She was an *activista* as a young woman. Helen's brother questioned what she was doing—and choked off the financial support for her education. Her fiery spirit could not be tamped down. Later Helen's *activismo* would liberate thousands of *Puertorriqueñas* on the island and many more women in the United States from policies and practices affecting their bodies, themselves, and their families.

Helen was born in New York City to Puerto Rican parents. But she spent her early years in Puerto Rico. When she was ten, her mother divorced her abusive husband and brought Helen to the mainland seeking an inspiring horizon. She graduated from the University of Puerto Rico, and later, against many odds, Helen earned her degree in medicine at the University of Puerto Rico as well. She became a doctor at age thirty-one, the same year she gave birth to her fourth child.

Helen wanted to be a physician because medicine "combined the things I loved the most, science and people." She completed her residency in pediatrics and started the first care center for newborns on the island, lowering the death rate by 50 percent in three years.

Criticized by her second husband for "wanting a career," in 1970 Helen divorced and left Puerto Rico for New York City "to become part of the women's movement." Women's issues in medicine were to become her focus for the rest of her career.

A new radical way of thinking fell upon Helen after viewing the movie *Blood of the Condor*, a story about the revolt of Ecuadorian women who had been sterilized without permission. How did it compare to women's health care in Puerto Rico? she was asked. After much reading she realized that she had been *"totally oblivious to the sterilization of women"* on the island; her research led her to discover that far too many women—mostly poor or with disabilities—had been sterilized without being fully informed.

"I HOPE I'LL see in my lifetime a Growing realization that we are one world."

Helen became a founding member of the Committee to End Sterilization Abuse. Later in her life she testified in front of the Department of Health, Education, and Welfare advocating for guidelines she had drafted.

Women have the individual *right* of

choice regarding birth control and how many children to have, she believed. Rather than coercion, women deserved options "built into health programming," information in their language, and before any procedure, a "cooling-off period." Helen was on the way to pioneering a health revolution for Latinas; at the same time broadening the thinking in the mostly white women's movement.

There was never a question in her mind that she wanted to pursue community medicine, and in the 1970s she went to work in the largely Puerto Rican underserved neighborhood in the South Bronx. She headed up the pediatrics department at Lincoln Hospital, and as she treated children she was able to involve health care for their mothers and improve families' access to care. She believed that issues of social change—helping people make their lives better— were inextricably linked with better health care.

Helen informed women about health hazards, lead paint, and unprotected windows; she understood what was needed and reached out to all. In the late '80s she took on AIDS as an issue, with special attention to the needs of women with HIV. Her participation and leadership in the women's movement earned her deep respect.

At the age of sixty-four, as the first Latina President of the American Public Health Association, Dr. Helen Rodriguez-Trias reflected on what she had been fighting for her whole career: "We cannot achieve a healthier us without achieving a healthier, more equitable health care system, and ultimately, a more equitable society."

DOLORES HUERTA

*B*ORN: APRIL 10, 1930, IN DAWSON, NEW MEXICO

"Siete lenguas—seven tongues" grandfather Herculano Chavez called young Dolores—the girl who could propose, proclaim, declare, debate, inspire, challenge, and even pray—at lightning speed. She would one day conquer with words the giants of agribusiness, in the name of California's farmworkers.

Dolores was born in the mining town of Dawson, New Mexico, but after her parents divorced, Dolores's *familia* moved to Stockton, California, at the northern tip of the agricultural belt of the state, where her mother purchased and ran two hotels. Dolores noticed how she offered room and board, at no cost, to the local *campesinos* (farmworkers) with little food and no shelter. Mamá Alicia enrolled her jumpy, talky daughter in dance classes, piano lessons, and the school choir.

At school, Dolores, a budding poet, excelled in her reports and papers. However, one teacher stamped a red "C" on her "A" work. "You don't have the brains for this," he mumbled.

Dolores opened a Teen Center while at Stockton High, winning support from the locals—until the police boarded it up. How could whites mix with African Americans and Mexicans? Competing for the trophy given to whoever sold the most World War II bonds to support the troops, *"Siete lenguas"* won. She was denied the prize.

How could a Mexican girl accomplish such a feat? the sponsors said.

After graduating from University of the Pacific with a teaching credential (the first in her family to attend college), she decided she could do more by speaking for and organizing farmworkers than by teaching their children.

"It was a pot of gold!" Dolores said when she began doing community organizing with Fred Ross, who had started the Community Service Organization (CSO) in order to battle segregation, fend off police brutality, kick-start voter registration drives, and improve public services in general. Dolores opened a chapter in Stockton, then created the Agricultural Workers Association (AWA) to lobby government legislators in Sacramento for farmworkers' rights.

Dolores expanded her vision—farmworkers needed the removal of citizenship requirements from pension and public assistance programs for legal residents of California and the United States. They needed the right to vote in Spanish and to take the driver's license exam in their native language. Dolores raised her voice and led others to help make these changes happen.

Dolores met César Chávez, another community organizer, while working in the CSO. Both deeply believed in solving the injustices that farmworkers faced. After leaving the CSO in the early sixties, César and Dolores created the National Farm Workers Association (NFWA) in Delano, California, in the heart of the San Joaquin Valley. On September 16, 1965, the NFWA joined the Agricultural Workers Orga-

"¡sí, se puede!"
"yes, we can!"

nizing Committee (an outgrowth of the AWA that Dolores had started a few years earlier) in a strike where over five thousand grape workers walked off their jobs for better pay and working conditions. These efforts were followed by more successful negotiations that Dolores conducted on behalf of the farmworkers. Dolores worked with César Chávez for over thirty years until he died in 1993.

In 1966, Dolores debated, spoke for, and worked out the NFWA contract with the Schenley Wine Company, the first time that such a corporation negotiated with a group of organized farmworkers. With intense determination and unrelenting valor, Dolores continued making such landmark changes in labor policy for the next four decades.

One of her most successful calls for boycotts resulted in the enactment of the California Agricultural Labor Relations Act of 1975. This law granted farmworkers the right to collectively organize and bargain for better wages and working conditions.

Dolores organized field strikes, directed the grape, lettuce, and Gallo Wine boycotts, and led farmworkers in campaigns for political candidates. Her communication style was forceful and uncompromising. With this talent, she succeeded in bringing together many community workers, religious groups, students, peace groups, feminists, and Hispanic associations.

For her tireless work on behalf of farmworkers, in 2012 Dolores Huerta was awarded the Medal of Freedom from President Obama whose campaign slogan—"Yes, we can!"—was an echo of the words of Dolores Huerta: *"¡Sí, se puede!"* "Yes, we can!"

Jaime Alfonso Escalante

BORN: DECEMBER 31, 1930, IN LA PAZ, BOLIVIA
DIED: MARCH 30, 2010, IN ROSEVILLE, CALIFORNIA

High on the plateaus of the Bolivian *altiplano,* skinny Jaime collected and wound torn tire strips into a tight ball. Then he slammed it against a wall to win at one his favorite games—*frontón,* handball. He loved to compete. And he loved math.

Jaime competed *with himself*—to stay alive and positive. He worked at every spelling game his maternal grandfather José tossed him. His parents had been sent by the government to teach in the Aymara and Quechua Indian villages, but when Jaime was nine, his mother decided to return to La Paz, where he had been born.

At the elementary school in the city, other students laughed at his clothes—he wore Aymara fire-colored long-sleeved shirts, like the *aguayo* weavings in the Inca villages. But Jaime fired back with his arithmetic skills and basketball, soccer, and handball moves.

By the time he was fourteen, his mother scratched up enough money to enroll agile Jaime into the prestigious San Calixto Jesuit High School where he devoured advanced books on physics. He was a popular math whiz and a wiry street fighter—and a prankster shooting firecrackers under a professor's gown at graduation.

Because his mother could not afford engineering school, Jaime went on to earn a teaching credential, and by 1961, he had become a successful math teacher. He told his students: *"Lo mediocre no sirve,"* "Mediocrity is worthless." He challenged them to be fearless. He tried new approaches and if something didn't work, he changed his methods.

Then he made a decision for himself. Jaime told his wife, Fabiola, "I cannot progress here. I am going to America and I am going to start from zero."

Two years later, he left the family for one year, then brought them to Los Angeles where he had found work mopping floors and being a short-order cook. He had to start his college career all over again in the United States. For ten years, he focused on his evening classes at Pasadena Community College in order to obtain a college degree and a teaching credential as he worked a second job as an electronics tech. Then Jaime was ready to leap into teaching again.

He got a job at East LA's Garfield High School. It was in a tough neighborhood. Students were unmotivated and often absent. Jaime's idea was to tell his students in as many ways as possible that "one of the greatest things you have in life is that no one else has the authority to tell you what you want to be." His new idea was about self-respect, to put in hard work, to have *ganas,* the *inspiring desire,* to learn and to make your dreams happen. "If you have a negative image of yourself, you really kill yourself."

"TEACHING IS TOUCHING LIFE."

But first, Kimo, as the students called him, had to conquer the low expectations of the faculty and students. After heated arguments, Jaime convinced the school administration that Garfield students had potential and that no one should be satisfied with weak mathematics skills. He pushed the school to purchase math books that included algebra, trigonometry, and advanced math. Room 241, Jaime's calculus coliseum, was the battleground for success. Growing numbers of students enrolled in his class. Kimo became a master of motivation.

By 1982, AP Calculus, the hardest math class offered in high schools, was bursting with eighteen students. Kimo conducted SAT drills, after-school work meetings, work during lunch, and extra sessions for more prep tests. Even parents had to sign a contract. The kids were ready for the AP Calculus test administered by the ETS (Educational Testing Service), a national test.

Everyone passed. But the ETS was suspicious of these scores. No inner-city school had ever attained such scores. They were accused of cheating. Jaime, in turn, accused the test evaluators of racism; he felt that they could not accept that Latino barrio youth could succeed in advanced math. The heftiest challenge was not in Jaime's hands; the students had to determine their own fate, their own image of themselves. "Am I a winner or a loser?" The summer passed. So the ETS administered another test with just one week to prepare. All who took it passed.

In 1998, Jaime's life story became the basis of the feature film *Stand and Deliver*. Jaime Escalante competed for everyone—and won.

Rita Moreno

BORN: DECEMBER 11, 1931, IN HUMACAO, PUERTO RICO

"I finally got a chance . . . to play a real Hispanic person, . . . someone with character and strength!" said Rita Moreno about her 1962 Oscar-winning role in *West Side Story*. By then she had been in over twenty films. Rita held that Oscar up high, like the Statue of Liberty grasping the torch.

Rosa Dolores Alverio came from a family of *jíbaros*, small independent rural farmers in Puerto Rico. During the Great Depression, Rosa's mother left for New York City to work in the garment industry and took her daughter, known as Rosita, along. Rosita missed her little brother and father, and her homeland, and she didn't speak any English. There wasn't any extra money, but her mother enrolled her in dance classes because Rosita really wanted to learn to dance.

When Rosita was seven, she made her first public appearance, dancing at a nightclub in Greenwich Village. During the day she would struggle to learn English at school, and at night she took acting and dance classes and went to auditions. At the age of thirteen, Rosita landed her first role on Broadway.

Soon enough Rosita caught the attention of Hollywood talent scouts. This led to more professional song and dance shows and her first film, *So Young, So Bad*. Still a teenager, she shortened her first name, changed her last name, and became Rita Moreno.

Even though she was getting public exposure, Rita was not happy with the casting roles where she had to dance barefoot, make pouty and sulky faces, and act sultry. Then the big break came—a chance to audition for *West Side Story*. She tried out for the role of Anita, the strong, willful older sister who is the head of the family. There was not one, but three auditions—in acting, singing, and dancing. "The thing that scared me the most was dancing, because I hadn't danced at that time for at least ten years!" Rita registered for dance classes before the audition. Trying to get her groove back, she rehearsed jazz dance eight hours a day until the audition. Rita won the role, and then she won the Oscar. She had come a long way.

"Once I had that little gold man [the Oscar] in my grasp, I thought, okay, that's it—no more of those stereotypical Conchita-Lolitas." But Rita was not offered a serious role and did not make a major film for the next seven years. "I just couldn't believe that I wasn't getting any offers," she said.

So she turned to acting onstage and performed in London and New York. It was one place where people of color could reach for the stars and just maybe catch one. Television was another option—*The Muppets*, *The Bill Cosby Show*, *The George Lopez Show*. In the seventies she focused her talents on children's shows, appearing on *Sesame Street* and *The Electric*

"THere were no role models. I was my own role model—myself."

58

Company. Rita's mission was to inspire Hispanic children. When interviewed at the time she mentioned how alone she had felt as a child because she was different, and she wanted the new generations of children to feel positive about their identities. Rita told the media proudly that she was Latina and knew what it felt like to be different.

By the end of the '70s Rita Moreno's dream came true. Measuring five feet and two and half inches, she became one of the all-time great Puerto Rican entertainers—the only female artist to win the four major entertainment awards: an Oscar, a Tony, a Grammy, and two Emmys. When her star was unveiled on the Hollywood Walk of Fame, Rita fell on it, weeping—"I had been dreaming of this day since I was six."

Rita Moreno's life and career were not merely lists of outstanding work and dazzling awards in the performing arts. Rita continued to cross boundaries and to break borders—not for herself—but for others, young people in particular. For Latino children and youth, she became a new positive figure, a multitalented, authentic model of creative action.

In June of 2004, President George W. Bush awarded Rita Moreno the Presidential Medal of Freedom. She was acknowledged as a great artist and a pioneer in her ability to go beyond the early discriminatory practices of Hollywood.

ROBERTO CLEMENTE

BORN: AUGUST 18, 1934, IN CAROLINA, PUERTO RICO
DIED: DECEMBER 31, 1972, OFF THE COAST OF SAN JUAN, PUERTO RICO

"Respeto, **have respect, Roberto!** *Clemencia,* be merciful." These are words Roberto Clemente's parents counseled him. He was born in the barrio in Carolina, Puerto Rico, and lived in a small house made of whitewashed wood planks threaded with corn leaves with his six siblings and three cousins. For the rest of his life, Roberto was fueled by his hard beginnings and a will to stand up for a higher cause.

Outside, by the cane fields, young Roberto practiced baseball—with tomato cans, string balls, and baseballs made out of rags. By the time he was in high school, he was already a shortstop for a top amateur team in Carolina.

In 1954, at nineteen years, 5'11" and 174 pounds, he signed with the Montreal Royals, a farm club of the Brooklyn Dodgers. The talented Roberto was a bench player to keep him away from the Giants, who already had Willie Mays. But it was the Pittsburgh Pirates who signed him the next year. He played his entire major league career with the Pirates.

On the field, Roberto had no mercy. He charged tough, ran like thunder in a crouched position, scooped the ball, exploded into the air, and blasted overhand pegs to the plate. He galloped around the bases, like a horse. "His body was a baseball machine," said a teammate. And when Willie Mays slammed the ball to the right-field corner, Clemente crashed into the unpadded brick and cut a six-stitch gash on his chin—but the ball was owned by Mr. Roberto Clemente.

Respeto did not come easy. And it required having a stadium-sized voice. To the sportswriters, he spoke up against being quoted in choppy "broken" English, for being called a "hot dog." "I attack [the press] strongly, because since the first Latino arrived in the big leagues he was discriminated against without mercy!" He detested being told where to sit, eat, sleep.

Respeto did not come fast. A decade after Jackie Robinson broke the color bar in baseball, Roberto was kept on the bus with other players of color while white players stepped out for chow in White Only restaurants.

In every city his team visited during the eighteen seasons he played for the Pirates, Clemente spoke out: "I represent the poor people. I represent the common people of America. So I am going to be treated like a human being."

"IF YOU HAVE A CHANCE TO HELP OTHERS AND FAIL TO DO SO, YOU'RE WASTING YOUR TIME ON THIS EARTH."

In the hotels in the towns he visited, Roberto would organize children's fan mail and meet the children in hospitals. In the off-seasons, he went to Latin America, raising funds to help buy food, medicine, and sports equipment for children in poor neighborhoods, such as the one he had come from.

He strove *to be excellent every second,* every season. Even with food poisoning before the last game in his life, "Mr. Fury" put his knobless, 36-ounce bat to work—boom! He collected his 3,000[th] hit. In the 1971 World Series against the Orioles, who had a fourteen-game winning streak, he swung like a "man falling down a fire escape," and sped like a "broken windmill," every limb pumping and flying in all directions. Back at the dugout, Clemente soothed his team, "Hold on, we're gonna do it!" And they did—they won the series. In baseball, whether he was garnering the Most Valuable Player award (1966), the World Series MVP (1971), or winning twelve Gold Glove Awards in different years, he was "something close to the level of absolute perfection," wrote Roger Angell, a baseball writer for *The New Yorker.*

The final day of the season in 1972 would be his last major league game. On December 23 of that year, a huge earthquake devastated Nicaragua's capital, Managua. Roberto hurried and packed an aging DC-7 with 210 tons of clothing and 36 tons of food. On New Year's Eve, 1972, six minutes after takeoff, crackling, the plane drifted over Punta Muldonado and disappeared into the Atlantic.

The next year, Roberto Clemente was inducted posthumously into the Baseball Hall of Fame, becoming the first Latin American. He was also one of only two Hall of Fame members for whom the mandatory five-year waiting period was waived. Batting for humanity, Clemente stood tall for all.

TOMÁS RIVERA

ℬORN: DECEMBER 22, 1935, CRYSTAL CITY, TEXAS
𝒟IED: MAY 16, 1984, IN FONTANA, CALIFORNIA

In the Tomás Rivera Library at the University of California, Riverside, there are photographs and documents that trace the chapters of the life of the man who was a pioneering educator, trailblazing writer, and became the first Hispanic chancellor in the University of California system.

The son of migrant farmworkers, his *familia* followed the harvests from Texas to Minnesota and back again. In his treks through Michigan with his family, hungry for work in the beet fields, Tomás listened to stories in the labor camps. Like the other Mexican migrants, they were "always moving, always searching ... never giving up and dying."

On those unpredictable routes, Tomás met the "library lady" in Hampton, Iowa. Walking to the post office, a librarian noticed him and invited him into the building. "It was the first time I had ever come in contact with a library. . . . I didn't even know what 'Carnegie Library' meant." "What do you want to know?" she asked. Everything was the answer. Tomás voraciously read books on Africa and other countries, mystery writers, and endless collections on sports. His father knocked on doors asking for magazines for his son. The two would venture to the town dump, picking out Tomás's select "dump collection." With an encyclopedia, "You could just read one thing after another," he said.

When Tomás was about twelve, he decided he was going to be a writer. His writing would be about the world he had so far experienced; he would become a "documenter" of the lives of the migrants, and all "those without any protections."

Back in Texas for high school, in a segregated school, he was determined to graduate, even though he and his family were still migrants and often did not return home in time for the opening of the school year. He went on to college at Southwest Texas State University, where in his last year he came upon a book in the library: *With His Pistol in His Hand,* by Américo Paredes.

In the Paredes volume, Tomás recognized the *corridos,* the storytelling ballads of the heroic rebel, Gregorio Cortez. He had sung them in the migrant camps as the *migrantes* shared songs and acted out stories after a long day's work. He became aware that "it was possible for a Chicano to publish." And ". . . that it was possible to talk about *a Chicano as a complete figure.*" Tomás knew he had seen a lot of heroic people, and wanted to capture their feelings, and to portray a positive image as opposed to a negative one.

"IF YOU WANT TO WRITE, YOU HAVE TO HAVE A LOVE FOR PEOPLE."

He graduated from college but had difficulty finding a teaching job in San Antonio as no one wanted to hire a Mexican. After receiving a master's degree in Education in 1964, Tomás taught English and Spanish in high schools and went on to get a second master's degree in Spanish Literature.

In 1969, he received his PhD in Romance Languages from the University of Oklahoma at Norman.

Tomás published his first book in 1970, *Y no se lo tragó la tierra, And the Earth Did Not Devour Him,* written in the poetic voice of a migrant Mexican child. Published at the beginning of the Chicano literary explosion, he won the first UC-Berkeley Quinto Sol National Literary Prize. He published a collection of poems a few years later, *Always and Other Poems.* Tomás was also known for his short stories and many essays on education, writing, and Chicano literature.

In 1971 Tomás became a professor of Spanish at the University of Texas, San Antonio. And in 1979 he was appointed as chancellor at the University of California, Riverside, the youngest ever and the first minority chancellor.

All along, in between papers, speeches, awards, and meetings in national organizations, being a founding member of the National Council of Chicanos in Higher Education and as a Board Trustee of the Carnegie Foundation for the Advancement of Teaching, in the emerging Chicano literary movement in the seventies, Tomás became an inspirational voice.

In his commencement speech at the University of California, Riverside, Tomás Rivera asked the student class of 1980 to "recollect" their lives, themselves, and reminded them that "from that remembrance will come forth the will to continue, to survive . . . to be, again and again." He had dedicated his life to opening doors for so many of them.

joan baez

BORN: JANUARY 9, 1941, IN NEW YORK, NEW YORK

In 1959, eighteen-year-old Joan Chandos Baez nervously picked up her Goya guitar at the Newport Folk Festival. She unleashed her soprano voice and awakened the folk song movement, lifting the hearts of a new generation. It was a new time—she offered them electrifying words of hope, peace, and change.

By the age of ten, with her parents and her sisters, Pauline and Mimi, Joan had already lived in many places. She often felt lonely. Her mother gave her a copy of *The Diary of Anne Frank*. "It was lodged inside my heart and soul," she said. Joan began to ponder questions about justice and freedom.

In junior high, in Redlands, California, the melancholy-eyed girl with the Mexican name, skin, and hair, sang in the choir and was bullied for her different views. As a daughter of Quakers, Joan had attended Quaker work camps, listened to arguments about "alternatives to violence," and talked about the Cold War and the arms race. Classmates avoided her. One summer she picked up a ukulele, trained herself all that season, and changed her "sweet . . . thin and straight" voice into a vibrant, magnetic cascade. "Powerless to change my social standing, I decided to change my voice," she said.

69

In 1954, living in Palo Alto, California, Joan heard Pete Seeger, a folk song pioneer, with his banjo and his high-pitched conversations on workers' rights. Three years later, at a conference organized by the Quakers, she listened to a young Dr. Martin Luther King Jr. speak about fighting injustice with "weapons of love"—nonviolent acts like boycotts and "walking to freedom." Joan stood up, cheering and crying. Now, Joan's voice had purpose—to help bring about equality, peace, and unity.

The family moved again, this time to Cambridge, Massachusetts, after her father, Albert Baez, accepted a teaching position at MIT. In Boston, Joan began to sing in coffeehouses, tiny stages with rough, brick walls, cinnamon-apple cider, and cigarette smoke filtering through the half-lit cafés. In this atmosphere, with college youth longing for *change* as she did, she recorded her first album. It was 1960, a year after her appearance at the Newport Folk Festival. Her soulful, soprano voice, her kind, deep, dark eyes, and her brave speeches on nonviolence helped inspire a movement.

Other young folksingers, like Bob Dylan and Phil Ochs, finger-pickin' their six strings and blowin' into their "harps," made the rounds, too. Bob Dylan was a scruffy songwriter sizzling with new songs. "It was as if he was giving voice to the ideas I wanted to express, but didn't know how," Joan said of him. She invited the unknown Dylan to go on tour with her and became a songwriter in her own right.

Hearing her songs, Dr. Martin Luther King Jr.

"ALL SERIOUS DARING STARTS FROM WITHIN."

invited her to the March on Washington. It was 1963. At the march, arm in arm with Martin Luther King, Joan sang "We Shall Overcome." Her heart strengthened, her voice opened like a rainbow. Joan became a lead figure of the Civil Rights Movement.

And she kept on marching. Along with a friend, she set up the Institute for the Study of Nonviolence in Carmel, California, in order to teach "Peace Studies." With her mother, Joan was imprisoned for forty-five days at the Santa Rita Rehab Center for blocking doorways of the Armed Forces Induction Center in Oakland, California. In 1972, during the Vietnam War, Joan headed to North Vietnam on a peace mission to bring mail to POWs. Joan sang, "No more bombing, Lord, save the children, Lord . . . "

Throughout the years, Joan kept on recording, with more than fifty albums since 1960; she used her songs to "defend whoever is in the right." Her voice soared in Sarajevo at the height of the shelling during the Bosnian War for Independence; rang through audiences in Argentina and Chile in support of the mothers of *Los Desaparecidos*; and as she stood with Lech Walesa in Poland and Vaclav Havel in Czechoslovakia for freedom from Soviet invasions.

Joan Baez's gliding, golden voice sings for all time. Her heart is blazing with life.

JUDITH F. BACA

Born: September 20, 1946, in Los Angeles, California

Alone in the corner of her kindergarten class, Judy was allowed to do an art assignment since she could not speak English. She poured out her heart with paints.

At home, in Watts barrio, Los Angeles, a place of turnip fields and trolleys in the early 1950s, Judy poured out her dreams to her grandmother Francisca. For Judy's early life, it was an all-women family of her grandmother, two aunts, and her mother, Ortencia, who had migrated from Colorado to Los Angeles after World War II to work in a factory to support *la familia.*

But Judy's *familia* changed when her mother remarried and they moved to Pacoima, another area of the city. By middle school time, in Pacoima, Judy was a rebellious little girl who was taunted in school. She was the "odd girl," the "Mexican girl," the "fighting girl." To head off trouble, her mother transferred her to the Catholic Bishop Alemany High School.

The nuns encouraged Judy. She tackled her studies, excelled in art, and went on to college. In 1969, she received her BA from Cal State University at Northridge and, although she wanted to be an artist, she decided to teach art. Sister Luisa Bernstein at Bishop

Alemany High offered her a job at her old high school.

There she first tried out her idea of combining art and community. She set up an Allied Arts program for ninth graders where they could examine history and current issues like the Vietnam War in the open air with art, poetry, and music. She got ethnically diverse students to paint a mural, anticipating the way she would come to connect art and social action. But Judy was fired from her teaching job along with several nuns and teachers for participating in an anti–Vietnam War protest. She didn't know if she would get another job teaching art. Then a new door opened. The Parks and Recreation Program hired her to teach arts—not in school, but in the parks. Her first job took her to the Boyle Heights barrio of East Los Angeles, an area divided by rival gangs.

"Hey, art lady, show us your art," the tough youth hollered. "I will, if you show me yours first," Judy said. Soon enough, with her teaching skills and what she knew from growing up in Watts and Pacoima, she had teens from four different neighborhoods working in teams on art projects. They called themselves, *Las Vistas Nuevas,* "the New Horizons." When she had set off for college, her mother told her: "Do something that will make a difference." Judy believed that art could be used to help children improve their lives.

"STEP OUT OF THE environment you are in and see from higher ground."

Las Vistas Nuevas grew to become a city-wide mural program, with participants creating more than four hundred murals over the years. Judy was an artist just as she had dreamed—but she was a public artist. "I chose not to make art that people could collect in private and decide who gets to see it. My work was in public space for everyone to see it." And the mural was the art form she made. She traveled to Mexico to study the great Mexican muralist, Diego Rivera. Back in Los Angeles she painted alongside the young people she was helping.

In 1974, at the peak of the Chicano Arts Movement, the Army Corps of Engineers approached Judy about improving the area around a San Fernando Valley flood control channel. In place there was a long blank concrete wall. *What if all the people I have been working with in all the different communities came to one site and created a piece together?* she wondered. For five summers the "mural makers" stretched their imagination and immigrant realities painting candles, battles, and rainbow-haired women on the "Great Wall of Los Angeles." It stretches a half mile—the longest mural in the world. The mural is called *La Memoria de Nuestra Tierra*, Our Land of Memory, and it depicts an "unofficial" history of California, which includes Native Americans, women, and minorities. Judy calls this mural one of the largest monuments to interracial harmony.

In 1976, she founded her own nonprofit arts organization—Social and Public Art Resource Center (SPARC). It promotes community-based public arts projects, and helps to preserve the murals painted all over Los Angeles. She became a professor at the University of California in Irvine, then in Los Angeles. Now with her students at UCLA, Judy reminds them, "See further and dream larger."

sonia sotomayor

BORN: JUNE 25, 1954, IN NEW YORK, NEW YORK

Her mother and father called little Sonia *Ají*—hot chili pepper—because she was always jumping around and tumbling through her family's tiny apartment in the South Bronx section of New York City.

Sonia could not stand still—jousting as a knight with her younger brother, Juli, and even acting out spooky voices at her grandmother Mercedes's *espiritista* séances. Sonia was blistering energy. At Blessed Sacrament school she would protect her brother, "and any bully thinking of messing with him would have to mix it up with me first," she said. When her father nervously attempted to give her the first insulin injection for her diabetes, he squirted the needle over her shoulder by accident, and the seven-year-old Sonia grabbed the needle and popped it into her arm. Later she recalled, "The only way I'd survive was to do it by myself."

"Do it by myself!"—This was the spirit and determination that marked the child Sonia from the start. And it carried through to debate competitions at school, exacting tests at Princeton and Yale Law School, and combative trials in the courtroom as assistant district attorney, then judge, and finally Supreme Court justice.

From an early age Sonia Sotomayor embraced life with all its pain, challenges, and *spice*. Her *abuelita* took Sonia to the island of Puerto Rico, where they strolled through the neighborhoods savoring coconut milk, *tembleques,* and guavas, and her *abuelita*'s spontaneous lilting poems. Always observant, when Sonia returned to New York she noticed that unlike the island there were no Puerto Rican managers or directors or owners of businesses. *Puertorriqueños* on the mainland, like her father, worked hard and rarely were promoted. Often the jobs were temporary.

Sonia decided to shield herself from all this with books. At home she read *Highlights* magazine and her mama's *Reader's Digest.* Sonia barreled into the *Encyclopedia Britannica* her mother ordered. She gobbled newspaper articles and joined the Forensics debate team at school, writing down lists of new words and argument strategies. She read every Nancy Drew novel she could get her hands on, and decided that she wanted to be like Nancy Drew. Or even better, to be like Nancy's father, the judge, because the judge called the shots. On her black-and-white TV, she was moved by Pope Paul VI's speech in the fall of 1965 when he mentioned the destinies of people and of all mankind. Maybe words and how you offer them can make a difference, she thought. So, Sonia volunteered to be a bible reader at church to help her learn to speak persuasively in front of an audience.

Sonia applied to Princeton University. Even though she had been at

"AS YOU DISCOVER WHAT STRENGTH YOU CAN DRAW FROM YOUR COMMUNITY . . . LOOK OUTWARD AS WELL AS INWARD. BUILD BRIDGES INSTEAD OF WALLS."

the top of her class and won an Affirmative Action scholarship, she quickly realized she had little to work with in that new academic culture. She headed to the library. "I planned with each course to gulp down as much as I could. I was aware of my needs," she said.

An active member of *Acción Puertorriqueña,* a student organization at Princeton, Sonia organized a bilingual volunteer team of students to help at the Trenton Psychiatric Hospital by translating for the Spanish speakers. They took turns at the hospital assisting patients and staff and making sure everyone understood what was taking place. The world of public service electrified her. It became Sonia's new purposeful world. Sonia graduated summa cum laude and received the Moses Taylor Pyne Prize, which was the highest honor for a Princeton graduating senior.

Sonia had already decided to be a lawyer *in service of the people.* In 1976, Sonia was accepted to Yale Law School and soon published in *The Yale Law School Journal* a lengthy "note" on Puerto Rico's powers to retain its seabed mineral rights. But a lawyer must be brave and must know how to move inside the "jaws of a huge, complex, and fast moving machine." Three years later, Sonia became the first Latina assistant district attorney for New York County. The word purpose still guided her. But she took joy that she was "working to improve it [the system], rather than enforcing it at the front lines."

In 1992, Sonia was elected a judge of the U.S. District Court, Southern District of New York, and in 1998 judge on the U.S. Court of Appeals for the Second Circuit. Then in 2009, Sonia Sotomayor was nominated by President Obama as the first Latina associate justice of the Supreme Court.

ELLEN OCHOA

BORN: MAY 10, 1958, IN LOS ANGELES, CALIFORNIA

When she was in fifth grade, Ellen was already setting goals: "I wanted to be class president." Even though her mother raised the family of five children by herself, she found time to instill in her children the courage to *take a leap* at an early age. Ellen's mother enrolled in college and took one class every semester while taking care of her children. "Mom didn't graduate until twenty-two years later, but she did finish," Ellen recalls. "That's what I got from her example. I've always liked school."

When Ellen graduated from high school in 1975, Stanford University immediately offered her a four-year scholarship, but she declined it so she could stay closer to home to help her family. She went to San Diego State University and graduated with a Bachelor of Science in Physics as valedictorian of her class with a perfect GPA. She went on to receive her doctorate in Electrical Engineering from Stanford, where she played the flute in the Stanford Symphony Orchestra.

When Ellen was not bicycling, playing volleyball, or earning her pilot's license, she was *propelled to learn.* Many different things caught her attention. Because of her many interests, ability to learn quickly, and her love for teamwork, Ellen was selected as a research engineer to work at the NASA Ames Research Center after graduation.

Ellen played with light beams, examined rays and electrons of lasers and holograms; with a team she became a co-inventor in the development of optical inspection systems. She supervised thirty-five engineer-scientists. Ellen's motto: "Only you put limitations on yourself about what you can achieve."

Ellen's next goal was to perform *scientific experiments in space,* using her inventions. But to go on a space mission, she needed to become an astronaut first. Growing up, it had never occurred to her. "When I was a girl, I never imagined being an astronaut," she said. "It wasn't until the first six female astronauts were selected in 1978 that women could even think of it as a possible career path." In 1983 Sally Ride became the first woman to travel into space. By this time, Ellen had graduated and was working at NASA, and she was inspired to do the same. Ellen had confidence about her strengths in many areas—engineering, music, flying planes, scientific inventions, and working in groups.

"I BELIEVE A GOOD EDUCATION CAN TAKE YOU ANYWHERE ON EARTH AND BEYOND."

Ellen was selected as an astronaut in January 1990. Training to become an astronaut is rigorous. She learned to scuba dive in a tank so she could experience weightlessness, to spacewalk, to fly in T-38 jets, and use robotic arms in a Shuttle training aircraft. "I was in training for three years before my first mission. Some astronauts have waited ten years, even sixteen."

¡Arriba! Up, up, up, up! In 1993, Ellen flew into space as a mission specialist aboard the Space Shuttle Discovery mission STS-56. On the nine-day mission, two hundred miles from earth, going five miles per second, she controlled the "robotic arm" and captured a satellite used for the study of the sun. Being an astronaut excited Ellen because "it allows you to learn continuously, like you do in school," she said.

Ellen zoomed into space on four space missions from 1993 to 2002. In each journey, with her team, she performed different maneuvers of increasing difficulty.

Out in space, Ellen marveled at Earth: "How beautiful and fragile it is." After a long day with the robotic arm maneuvering space walkers, Ellen added water to cookies, and ate dried fruit—and tortillas. Weightless, she did a front-flip while brushing her teeth. And then she e-mailed her husband and two children.

Dr. Ellen Ochoa, the first Latina astronaut, became the first Latina director of the Lyndon B. Johnson Space Center. She has worked toward human habitats on the moon and eventually, Mars. And she has a new goal: to establish summer camps for children like her, who never dreamed of riding the stars many moons ago.

Hero Street U.S.A.

As named in May 1967

Before it was renamed Hero Street USA in May 1967 by the mayor, and before a city park was built adjacent to that one-and-a-half-block-long path and dedicated in October 1971, it was simply called Second Street.

Second Street was on the west side of Silvis, Illinois, a Mississippi river town. It was little more than an unpaved muddy stretch between Honey Creek and Billy Goat Hill. But it was the home of eight American soldiers of Mexican descent who died in World War II and the Korean conflict of the early fifties. And as time clocked by, it became the proud street where more than one hundred and ten men and women had lived who served the United States of America. Recently, the Department of Defense in Washington, D.C., reported that there is no street of similar size where so many men and women left home in order to join the Armed Forces—eighty-four soldiers from twenty-six families who served in World War II, Korea, and Vietnam.

The street is alive with *familia*, courage, and memory.

The original Mexicans who settled in Silvis migrated from Guanajuato in the late 1920s and '30s in search of work. The Rock Island Railroad Line, needing labor nearby for track maintenance, set aside rent and tax-free plots of land with boxcar units as shift houses for cheap labor. But complaints were voiced regarding Mexicans living in rent-free boxcars.

So the Mexican community resettled in an unwanted area set aside for them by city officials. The boxcars were loaded on flatbed trailers and trucked over to their new location on an unpaved street—Second Street.

Twenty-two families with axes and machetes cleared the field and built their houses on both sides of Second Street. The migrant *Mexicanos* soon established Our Lady of Guadalupe Catholic Church and the *Corporación Mexican Band*.

As WWII began, the younger generation of Second Street joined the Navy, Marines, Air Corps, and the Army—forty-five fought in WWII and at least a dozen more in Korea. Eight never returned: Peter Masias, Tony Pompa, Claro Soliz, the Sandoval brothers—Frank and Joseph—Joseph Gomez, William Sandoval, and Johnny Munos.

The matriarch of Hero Street, Mrs. Angelina Sandoval, recalled her three sons who perished in the wars: "They didn't complain about going. This was their country, and they were willing to die for it." Frank Sandoval, the best slingshot shooter on Billy Goat Hill, was killed in Burma. Joseph Sandoval was overrun by Nazis. Santiago Sandoval made it home after being wounded in Korea, then, five weeks later, died in a car crash. Tony Pompa lied about his age to get into the Army Air Corps and flew tail gunner in a bomber that went down.

"THIS WAS THEIR COUNTRY, AND THEY WERE WILLING TO DIE FOR IT."

The unequal treatment continued for the

Mexican American soldiers who came home to Second Street after the war. For decades they were unwelcome at the original Silvis Veterans of Foreign Wars post, so they had to start their own meeting hall to hold ceremonies for Veterans Day. Determined that the war heroes would not be forgotten, some Mexican Americans from the town helped register people who would vote for supporters on the City Council. Joe Terronez, who later became the mayor of Silvis, proposed legislation that finally passed to pave Second Street and rename it Hero Street in 1967.

Guadalupe "Sonny" Soliz, whose uncle Claro Soliz died in Belgium in WWII, began to paint a series of thirteen watercolors depicting his street and its heroes. It took decades, but in 1993 the idea was born to organize with others to form the Hero Street Memorial Committee. Sonny became its chairman.

As planned, the monument would have the sculpted faces of the eight Hero Street soldiers cast in bronze. Steps would lead up from this level to a sculpture of a helmet hung with dog tags and topped with an M1 Garand rifle, a U.S. flag, and an eagle with outspread wings.

This monument was to be the main feature of a remodeled Hero Street Park. On November 12, 1997, the groundbreaking ceremonies began with a speech given by Louis Caldera, who became the Secretary of the Army. The monument arrived in Silvis on November 8, 2006— just in time for Veterans Day.

It commemorates the hometown heroes and the Medals of Honor that Latinas and Latinos throughout the nation have won in service of their country.

Victoria Soto was a twenty-seven-year-old first-grade teacher at Sandy Hook Elementary School in Newtown, Connecticut. She was shot shielding her students during the Newtown school shooting when the gunman burst into her classroom. She was among the six staff members and twenty children who died that day.

VICTORIA LEIGH SOTO

BORN NOVEMBER 4, 1985, IN BRIDGEPORT, CONNECTICUT

DIED DECEMBER 14, 2012, AT SANDY HOOK ELEMENTARY SCHOOL,

NEWTOWN, CONNECTICUT

SESTINA FOR
VICTORIA LEIGH SOTO
BELOVED TEACHER

Victoria, sister of Jillian, Carlee, and Carlos, you wanted to be a teacher
Daughter of Carlos, equipment operator, and Donna, nurse, one family
Since the beginning, at fourteen, Stratford High, your heart was strong
To learn, to explore, to collect the books, to map the road for others
A leader with heart, for all occasions, Christmas, baseball—for children
Long brown hair, blue eyes—we remember your smile and your strength

The world gathers since the fourteenth of December, with your strength
Form a circle with the stories of your bravery, everyone, every teacher
When the shots "pop-pop-popped" and bullets seared apart each family
How you shielded each one of your "sixteen angels" you stood up strong
You had prepared at Eastern and Southern each one a step for others
"One in a million," Chief MacNamara said, giving your life for children

Five years, you had taught at Sandy Hook, 27 years of age, the children
Said you were funny, you hugged everyone with your soul, your strength
The bagpipers played, four hundred came to mourn you—our teacher
Your love, your mind, your body, prepared to lead, to protect family
You hid your students in closets, in cabinets, what was it? Was it strong?
Newtown, Conn., the rest of us—how do we hold your gift for others?

89

Rev. Boxwell Williams said you were "selfless," but who are *our* "others"?
On Tumblr and FB we write about you, how we will follow you like children
A style for cheap sunglasses, Six Flags, the Yankees, we search for strength
Then we go back to Sandy Hook, offer flowers, each light a new teacher
Talking about becoming *Victorias,* victories, threading into one family
"The kids sensed her compassion," a father said, a renewing voice, strong

The bullets turned the hall as they burned, your teachers were strong
"It sounded like someone was kicking down the doors" onto the others
They went into lockdown they covered windows and sang to the children
Said, "I love you," under desks, bathrooms, storage rooms, quiet strength
Strips of paper, crayons, in the midst of terror, a drooling gun, a teacher
You faced the killer—"This is Victoria Soto," they said, now a family

December 14, 2012, dissolves, you are here, everywhere, with us, a family
"She walked the walk," a Navy veteran said about your teaching, strong
How you cared for first graders with different abilities, all the children
"She loved them automatically," the librarian said, this was your strength
"She was doing what she loved, protecting our children," this is a teacher
Cousin Jim Wiltsie, a Marine, said, ". . . she was a hero," voices of family

Voices sing your inner strength, your mother, Donna, father, Carlos, sisters
Brother, your life for flourishing children, family, the heart-steps of a teacher
for others, for Newtown, for us now, in the storm of fire, Victoria—
strength.

Source Notes

These notes provide the source for the main quotation that appears in color in each individual's section.

LUIS W. ALVAREZ

From his book *Alvarez: Adventures of a Physicist*. (New York: Basic Books, 1987)

DESI ARNAZ

From his book *A Book*. (New York: Morrow, 1976)

JUDITH F. BACA

From an interview with the author

JOAN BAEZ

From her book *And a Voice to Sing With: A Memoir*. (New York: Summit Books, 1989)

JULIA DE BURGOS

This quote is the title of one of de Burgos's most famous poems

CÉSAR ESTRADA CHÁVEZ

As quoted on the United Farm Workers website: http://www.ufw.org

DENNIS "DIONISIO" CHAVEZ

From *Everything You Need to Know About Latino History: 2008 Edition* by Himilce Novas. (New York: Plume, 2007)

ROBERTO CLEMENTE

From a speech Clemente gave as quoted in a PBS feature on him. A transcript can be found here: http://www.pbs.org/thinktank/transcript1247.html

JAIME ALFONSO ESCALANTE

From *Jaime Escalante: Inspirational Math Teacher* by Anne Schraff. (Berkeley Heights, NJ: Enslow Publishers, 2008)

DAVID GLASGOW FARRAGUT

From *Lincoln's Admiral: The Civil War Campaigns of David Farragut* by James P. Duffy. (Hoboken, NJ: John Wiley & Sons, 1997)

BERNARDO DE GÁLVEZ

From *I Alone : Bernardo de Gálvez and the Taking of Pensacola in 1781: A Spanish Contribution to the Independence of the United States* by Carmen de Reparaz, Translated by Walter Rubin. (Madrid: Ediciones de Cultura Hispánica, 1993)

HERO STREET, U.S.A.

From an interview with Sonny Soliz by the author

DOLORES HUERTA

As quoted on the United Farm Workers website: http://www.ufw.org

IGNACIO E. LOZANO

From an interview with Lozano's son by the author

RITA MORENO

From her book *Rita Moreno: A Memoir*. (New York: Celebra, 2013)

ELLEN OCHOA

From *Ellen Ochoa: First Latina Astronaut* by Lila

and Rick Guzmán. (Berkeley Heights, NJ: Enslow Publishers, 2006)

Adelina Otero-Warren

From *Nina Otero-Warren of Santa Fe* by Charlotte Whaley. (Santa Fe: Sunstone Press, 2007)

Tomás Rivera

From *Chicano Authors: Inquiry by Interview* by Juan Bruce-Novoa. (Austin: University of Texas Press, 1980)

Helen Rodriguez-Trias

As quoted on the Helen Rodriguez-Trias page on the National Library of Health website: https://www.nlm.nih.gov/changingthefaceofmedicine/video/273_1_trans.html

Sonia Sotomayor

From her book *My Beloved World*. (New York: Knopf, 2013)

ℬIBLIOGRAPHY

Luis W. Alvarez

Alvarez, Luis Walter. *Alvarez: Adventures of a Physicist*. New York: Basic Books, 1989.

"Luis Alvarez." Gale. Accessed December 12, 2010. http://www.gale.com/free_resources/chh/bio/alvarez_l.htm

Meier, Matt S., et al. "Luis W. Alvarez." *Notable Latino Americans*. Westport, CT: Greenwood Press, 1997.

Desi Arnaz

Arnaz, Desi. *A Book*. New York: Morrow, 1976.

Sandoval-Sánchez, Alberto. *José, can you see?: Latinos on and off Broadway*. Madison, WI: The University of Wisconsin Press, 1999.

Judith F. Baca

Baca, Judy. Telephone interview. August 21, 2013.

Baca, Judy. Accessed November 25, 2013. http://www.judybaca.com/now/index.php

Joan Baez

Baez, Joan. *And a Voice to Sing With: A Memoir*. New York: Simon and Shuster, 1987.

"Joan Baez in Conversation with Anthony DeCurtis at the 92nd Street Y." [Abridged] [Audible Audio Edition]. Joan Baez (Author), Anthony DeCurtis (Narrator). New York: 92nd Street Y, 2009.

Julia de Burgos

Burgos, Julia de. *Song of the Simple Truth: The Complete Poems of Julia de Burgos*. Translated by Jack Agüeros. Willimantic: Curbstone Press, 2008.

Meier, Matt S., et al. "Julia de Burgos." *Notable Latino Americans*. Westport, CT: Greenwood Press, 1997.

Roman-Odio, Clara. "Julia de Burgos." *Dictionary of Literary Biography*. Ed. Maria A. Salgado. 2nd ed. Vol. 290. Gale, 2004.

César Estrada Chávez

Levy, Jacques E. *Cesar Chavez: Autobiography of La Causa* (with a new postscript by the author). Foreword by Fred Ross Jr. Afterword by Jacqueline M. Levy. Minneapolis, MN: University of Minnesota Press, 2007.

Soto, Gary (and Laurie Lohstoeter). *Cesar Chavez: A Hero for Everyone*. New York: Alladin Paperbacks, 2003.

Dennis "Dionisio" Chavez

"Chavez, Dennis, 1888–1962." Bibliographical Directory of the United States Congress. Accessed July 27, 2013. http://bioguide.congress.gov/scripts/biodisplay.pl?index=c000338

Etulain, Richard W., Ed. *New Mexican Lives: Profiles and Historical Stories.* Albuquerque, NM: University of New Mexico Press, 2002.

Leonard, Kevin Allen. "Dennis Chavez: The Last of the Patrons." Wilmington: Scholarly Resources Inc., 2002.

Roberto Clemente

Maraniss, David. *Clemente: The Passion and Grace of Baseball's Last Hero.* New York: Simon and Schuster, 2006.

Jaime Alfonso Escalante

Matthews, Jay. *Escalante: The Best Teacher in America.* New York: Henry Holt and Company, 1988.

"Jaime Escalante: On Being a Teacher." The Futures Channel. Accessed December 12, 2013. http://www.youtube.com/watch?v=FFMz8JRg8Y8

David Glasgow Farragut

Spears, John Randolph. *David G. Farragut.* Philadelphia, PA: George W. Jacobs & Company, 1905.

"Admiral David Farragut." Virtualogy. Accessed July 9, 2009. http://www.virtualology.com/uscivilwarhall/ADMIRALFARRAGUT.ORG/

Bernardo de Gálvez

Caughey, John Walton, and Jack D. Holmes (Foreword). *Bernardo de Gálvez in Louisiana 1776–1783.* Gretna: LA: Pelican Publishing Company, 1972.

Roberts, Russell. *Bernardo de Gálvez (Latinos in American History).* Hockessin, DE: Mitchell Lane Pub, Inc., 2003.

Hero Street, U.S.A.

Soliz Sr., Sonny. Telephone interview (Hero Street Monument Committee). March 1, 2007.

"Artist presents Hero Street model." Hero Street USA. March 19, 2006. Accessed March 5, 2007. http://herostreetusa.org/art11.html

"Remembering Sacrifice." Hero Street USA. Accessed March 5, 2007. http://herostreetusa.org/art20.html

Dolores Huerta

Worth, Richard. *Dolores Huerta* (The Great Hispanic Series). New York: Chelsea House Pub., 2006.

"Dolores Huerta." Dolores Huerta Foundation. Accessed June 15, 2007. http://www.doloreshuerta.org/index.htm

"Dolores Huerta." Gale. Accessed May 2, 2007. http://www.gale.com/free_resources/chh/bio/huerta_d.htm

Ignacio E. Lozano

Ignacio Lozano Jr. Telephone interview. Feb. 21, 2007.

"History of La Opinión." *La Opinión.* May 10, 2007. http://www.laopinion.com/corporate/about/history/index.php?lang=en

Rita Moreno

Moreno, Rita. *Rita Moreno: A Memoir.* New York: Celebra, Penguin, 2013

"Puerto Rico Profile: Rita Moreno." *Puerto Rico*

Herald. March 23, 2006. Accessed August 15, 2008. http://www.puertorico-herald.org/issues/vol4n32/ProfileMoreno-en.html

ELLEN OCHOA

"Biography: Ellen Ochoa (and interview)" Scholastic. Accessed November 12, 2013 http://teacher.scholastic.com/activities/hispanic/ochoa.htm

"Biographical Data: Ellen Ochoa." National Aeronautics and Space Administration. Accessed February 2, 2012. http://www.jsc.nasa.gov/Bios/htmlbios/ochoa.html

"Johnson Space Center." Accessed October 24, 2013. http://www.nasa.gov/centers/johnson/home/#.UtWevf2d71p

ADELINA OTERO-WARREN

Ruiz, Vicki L. and Virginia Sanchez Korrol, eds. *Latina Legacies: Identity, Biography and Community (Viewpoints on American Culture)*. Oxford: Oxford University Press, 2005.

Adelina "Nina" Otero-Warren. Women of the West Musuem. Accessed April 7, 2012. http://theautry.org/explore/exhibits/suffrage/oterowarren_full.html

TOMÁS RIVERA

Bruce-Novoa, *Chicano Authors: Inquiry by Interview*. Austin, TX: University of Texas Press, 1980.

Lattin, Vernon E., Rolando Hinojosa, Gary D. Keller, eds. *Tomás Rivera, 1935–1984-: The Man and His Work*. Arizona: Bilingual Review Press, 1988.

Olivares, Julian, Ed. *Tomás Rivera: The Complete Works*. Houston: Arte Público, 1995.

Rivera, Tomás. *And the Earth Did Not Devour Him*. Houston: Arte Público Press, 1987.

HELEN RODRIGUEZ-TRIAS

Looper-Baker, Christina, and Baker-Kline, Christina, eds. "A Mother's Story: Helen Rodriguez-Trias." from *The Conversation Begins: Mother and Daughters Talk About Living Feminism*. New York: Bantam Books, 1996.

_____ "Helen Rodriguez-Trias," Interview by Tania Ketenjian from *The Conversation Begins: Mother and Daughters Talk About Living Feminism*. New York: Bantam Books, 1996.

Wilcox, Joyce. "The Face of Women's Health." Helen Rodriguez-Trías. *American Journal of Public Health*. June 2002. 92(6): 894. (Corrected by Am J PH). Accessed December 27, 2013. http://www.nlm.nih.gov/changingthefaceofmedicine/physicians/biography_273.html

SONIA SOTOMAYOR

Sotomayor, Sonia. *My Beloved World.* New York: Alfred A. Knopf, 2013.

Ada, Alma Flor. *Under the Royal Palms: A Childhood in Cuba*. New York: Atheneum Books, 1998.

Alarcón, Francisco X., and Maya Christina Gomez. *From the Bellybutton of the Moon: And Other Summer Poems / Del Ombligo de la Luna: Y Otros Poemas del Verano*. New York: Lee and Low Books, 2005.

Argueta, Jorge, and Elizabeth Gomez. *A Movie in My Pillow / Una Película en mi Amohada*. New York: Children's Book Press, 2001.

Belpré, Pura. *The Stories I Read to the Children: The Life and Writing of Pura Belpré, the Legendary Storyteller, Children's Author and NY Public Librarian*. New York: Centro Press, 2013.

Burgos, Julia de. *Song of the Simple Truth: The Complete Poems of Julia de Burgos*. translated by Jack Agüeros. Willimantic, CT: Curbstone Press, 1996.

Cruz, Celia, and Ana Cristina Reymundo. *Celia: My Life*. New York: Rayo, 2005.

Cumpian, Carlos, and Richard Leonard. *Poems About Latino Americans (Many Voices, One Song)*. New York: Children's Press, 1995.

Day, Frances Ann. *Latina and Latino Voices in Literature for Children and Teenagers*. Portsmouth, NH: Heinemann, 1997.

Engle, Margarita. *The Lightning Dreamer: Cuba's Greatest Abolitionist*. New York: HMH Books for Young Readers, 2013.

Engle, Margarita. *Silver People: Voices from the Panama Canal*. New York: HMH Books for Young Readers, 2014.

Flores-Galbis, Enrique. *90 Miles to Havana*. New York: Square Fish, 2012.

Garza, Hedda. *Latinas: Hispanic Women in the United States*. Albuquerque: University of New Mexico Press, 2001.

Jiménez, Francisco. *Reaching Out*. New York: HMH Books for Young Readers, 2009.

Krull, Katherine, and Yuyi Morales. *Harvesting Hope: The Story of Cesar Chavez*. New York: HMH Books for Young Readers, 2003.

Manzano, Sonia. *The Revolution of Evelyn Serrano*. New York: Scholastic Press, 2012.

Martínez, Rúben. *Crossing Over: A Mexican Family on the Migrant Trail*. New York: Picador, 2002.

Martinez, Victor. *Parrot in the Oven: Mi Vida*. New York: Rayo, 2004.

Matthews, Jay. *Escalante: The Best Teacher in America*. New York: Henry Holt and Company, 1988.

Miller, Debra A. *Dolores Huerta, Labor Leader*. Farmington Hills, MI: Lucent Books, 2006.

Mora, Pat, and Raúl Colón. *Tomás and the Library Lady*. New York: Dragonfly Books, 2000.

Otero-Warren, Adelina. *Old Spain in Our Southwest*. Santa Fe: Sunstone Press, 2007. (Originally published in 1936).

Rivera, Tomás, and Julián Olivares, ed. *Tomás Rivera: The Complete Works*. Houston: Arte Publico Press, 1998.

Stavans, Ilan, and Lalo Alcaraz, Illustrator. *Latino USA: A Cartoon History (Revised Edition)*. New York: Basic Books, 2012.

Tafolla, Carmen. *What Can You Do With a Rebozo?* New York: Tricycle Press, 2008.

Vega, Marta Moreno. *When the Spirits Dance Mambo: Growing up Nuyorican in El Barrio*. New York: Three Rivers Press, 2004.

Winter, Jeanette. *Biblioburro: A true story from Colombia*. New York: Beach Lane Books, 2010